YOUR KNOWLEDGE HAS VALUE

- We will publish your bachelor's and
  master's thesis, essays and papers

- Your own eBook and book -
  sold worldwide in all relevant shops

- Earn money with each sale

Upload your text at www.GRIN.com
and publish for free

Bibliographic information published by the German National Library:

The German National Library lists this publication in the National Bibliography; detailed bibliographic data are available on the Internet at http://dnb.dnb.de .

Imprint:

Copyright © 2017 GRIN Verlag
Print and binding: Books on Demand GmbH, Norderstedt Germany
ISBN: 9783668787155

This book at GRIN:

https://www.grin.com/document/438062

Syed Hassan Shah

Perspectives of Cooperative Caching

GRIN Verlag

GRIN - Your knowledge has value

Since its foundation in 1998, GRIN has specialized in publishing academic texts by students, college teachers and other academics as e-book and printed book. The website www.grin.com is an ideal platform for presenting term papers, final papers, scientific essays, dissertations and specialist books.

Visit us on the internet:

http://www.grin.com/

http://www.facebook.com/grincom

http://www.twitter.com/grin_com

Perspectives of Cooperative Caching (CC)

Index

Perspectives of Cooperative Caching (CC)

Engr. Syed Hassan Shah

Shaheed Zulfikar Ali Bhutto Institute of Science and Technology Dubai, UAE

Abstract

From the recent studies we come to know that the cooperative caching can improve the performance of system in wireless P2P networks such as hoc networks and mesh networks do. Somehow these all very high level studies leave many design and implementation issues which are still unanswered. While by study it shows that cooperative caching not only reduce the overhead copying issue between the user space and the kernel space, but it also allow data pipelines for end to end delay reduction. While the chip multiprocessors systems have made the on-chip caches as a decisive recourse shared among co-scheduled threads. Still there are many challenges with respect to design for limited bandwidth, increasing on-chip wire interruption and extra capability features. So effectively Cooperative cache can support minimizing average access of memory latency and inaccessibility of critical inter-thread interference. So Caching is the common technique used for improve the. Cooperative Cache approach is intended for the treatment of large video streams with on requires access. Day by day Mobile technology is coming around us. So for general this technology needs address of Internet Service Provider (ISP) for cross-domain traffic. So different researchers present's algorithms of the strategy that shows changes brought to the content center network protocol in to implement the method. As recent works on cooperative caching in networks technology like work on Content Center network also enables the manipulation of the cache resources of routers with new generation. For CRs mostly researcher proposed least recently Used (LRU) approach. Cooperative cache can improve accessibility of data objects in mobile ad hoc network, where a mobile host can communicate with any other system anywhere anytime. Cooperative caching in mobile technology brings reality with respect of peer to peer communication in which two systems can help on another in caching. From mobile support station they can retrieve data, but also realizing new dimensions for data caching in mobile technology. Different protocols are used to improve the cooperative cache replacement, cooperative cache admission control, management and accessibility of data.

Keywords: *Cooperative Cache (CC), least Recently Used (LRU),Point 2 Point (P2P), Internet Service Provider (ISP),Communication.*

1. Introduction

Caching is the key technique used to improve the retrieval of data of mobile client in mobile network technology. The recent widespread development of peer to peer (P2P) of wireless mobile communication technologies like IEEE 802.11 and other coupled the fact that computation power and storage of most mobile devices are improving in fast pace, A new information sharing paradigm known as P2P information access has rapidly taken change. The mobile clients can communicate among themselves to share information rather then having dependency on the connectivity to server [13]. As many researchers implemented the same technique of cooperative caching on the networks like web environment and all those implementations are the levels of system [2]. So for improving the access of data is done through cooperative caching technique gets importance [12]. Cooperative cache allows multiple nodes to share and coordinate data among themselves, can further explore the potential of caching technique [5]. This is a solution add another level to the storage of Hierarchy, It allows the client to access blocked cache by the other clients. This special technique is known as "Cooperative caching" which reduces the load of the server by allowing some of its local client's cache misses, handled by the other clients. Cooperative caching is different from other level of the storage hierarchy is that it distributed across the clients and it therefore shares its physical memory as the local caches of the client [1]. Similarly there is rapid growth in mobile communication technology. Mobile ad hoc Networks (MANETs) are the popular solution where you don't have network infrastructure. MANETs can be extended by connecting other devices that may be physically wired or in wireless network like Internet. In ad hoc networks, a mobile node communicates each other using multi-hop wireless interface [6]. Carrying mobile in work places like in public parks, university campus, markets, malls, airport terminals and other public spots get connected to Social Wireless Networks would be automatically formed by using the devices by ad hoc wireless connections. Those devices list includes Apple's iPhone, Google's, Androids, Amazons and other electronic vendors. Data enabled mobile devices present usage and wireless-enabled data applications have promoted in present mobile ecosystem new content broadcasting models have promoted usage in present data enabled mobile devices while using wireless enabled data applications. So giving free access to the local connected devices to share the server load and access the data and ignore the application cost of downloading and sharing such mechanism is also known as cooperative caching in wireless networks [7]. As with respect to hardware feature of microprocessor architects designed the Micro chips to improve the access and processing to get full control over data execution, so cache also have portion of key role in hardware point of view for chip micro processors that where logical accessing of data should be started [3]. So different perspectives of cooperative caching techniques used in ad hoc network, cooperative caching in mobile technology, cooperative caching in P2P mobile network, cooperative caching in wireless networks with multimedia sensors, Cooperative Caching in simple wireless/physical wired networks , cooperative caching design and implementation in P2p wireless networks and cooperative cache for chip multiprocessors are discussed.

1.1 Cache Definition

1.1.1 Caches as memory

A cache memory occasionally also called *RAM cache or cache storage;* it is a part prepared of very high-speed static rams (SRAM) instead of the dynamic RAM (DRAM) which are cheaper and slower before main memory. Caching memory is helpful since most of the programs occasionally access the similar data or information again and again. By keeping as all that of information in SRAM is to increase the speed of processing and computer avoids accessing the slower DRAM as show in the figure (a) mentioned below [14].

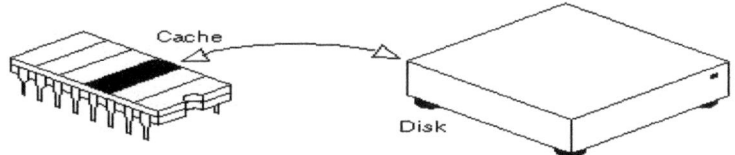

Figure (a) Cache is the part of disk to increase the speed of accessing [14].

1.1.2 Cache as hardware

Some of the cache memories are built into the structural design of microprocessors. Like the some of the Intel microprocessor contains i.e.a4K of memory cache and whiles the Pentiumhave8K cache. So the types of internal caches having such quality are often known as *Level one (L1) caches*. Most of the modern Personal Computers also have external cache memory, known as *Level two(L2) caches*. Such caches are placed between the Microprocessor and Dynamic RAM. Same as L-1 caches, L-2 caches are combined of Static RAM that is much larger [14].

1.1.3 Cache as supporting memory for processor

A CPU cache is known as a hardware cache used by the central processing unit of computer to decrease the regular cost in terms of time or energy to access data from internal memory. It is a faster memory, nearest to a micro processor, which can save the copies of the data that are frequently used by primary memory locations. The majority processors have different self-regulating caches, which includes data and instruction caches, while the cache used for data are usually managed as in order of more cache levels (L-1, L-2,----- L-n etc.) [15].

1.2. Cache Development

1.2.1 History

Cache memory was primary used on Personal Computers at the old timeframe systems that have time Microprocessor (CPU) did not itself hold cache memory inside to give support to motherboard. As the chip-set had a memory cache controller so that time the cache memory was outside to the CPU and thus also be optional. So main board without cache, the personal computers will be far-off slower than the personal computers having circuitry consists of cache. So now the controller used for cache memory in design known as "write-through," while for the write operations when the microprocessor wants to save information in memory the controller of cache memory will update the memory table in RAM instantaneously, so to increase the access speed [16].

1.2.2 Need

Cache for processor is keenly important in modern computers. Cache memory is one of the core elements for the difference in computers related to speed of transferring memory. Both the memory transfer rate and speed of calculation have impact in making difference in computers making them slower or faster. Faster calculation depends how much fast data fed into processor. The cycle will be missed if there is no data for processing and will wait for the next cycle for new data. To eliminate as much as possible about the wastage of cycle in necessary for processor to perform work fast.[17].

1.2.3 Implementation

Concept of the cache memory is to reduce memory access time. There may have long delays or even taking large number of cycles in memory accessing. By keeping data in local cache, so we can increase access time in a single clock cycle. So data and instruction locality is important, for fetching the next instruction going for execution. The memory is placed in cache to make processor ready for getting instruction easily and quickly [18].

1.2.4 Importance

As you here about the new processor coming into the market, the main point you focus maybe on the number of clock speed and how much cores it has. However some other factors which also affect the system performance in which one is the core element is cache. So question rises why does it have importance? Speed of the clock is what makes the processor faster and large number of cores generally anticipated to make demanding processor practically for applications as quicker as possible.

Similarly the cache is another important factor related to all processing speed. The cache can be added up in arithmetical arrangement, and size of it has a direct influence over all performance. Deprived of considering the size of cache of any processor, it is difficult to make a fully knowledgeable judgment about the upgrading next processor [19].

1.2.5 Group caching

Group Policy caching is thought to speed up the sign-in process for programs that are processed in synchronous mode during logon (Software Installation, Folder Redirection, Disk Quota, and Drive Mappings). The role of the cache comes only when you want synchronous processing in the mode of foreground. Which makes logic that synchronous processing can make the logo on processing significantly slow. So by using Group Policy setting in operating systems can make asynchronous process into running in foreground mode without enabling policy of synchronous group caching. For all that the concepts of understanding synchronous processing, asynchronous processing, foreground processing and background processing are must [20].

The use of group-caching also used in design in NOC centered multi-core cache-coherent machines, in which most of the researcher's uses on-chip L-2 banks which were organized to form numerous groups. Each of cache group works like a mutual L-2 cache for the cores inside cache group, whereas the cache-coherence among cache-groups is preserved by coherence messages. Group-caching also accepts the newly added cache replacement for improving the inefficient usage of the combined L-2 cache capability. Compared to banked and shared L2 design, as, Hopping count can considerably reduce by accessing most of L-2 caches functioned by native cache-group. So the study of most of researches shows that group-caching can also be used to increase the performance by some percentage associated to shared L-2 design and banked, with also some percentage reduced for network energy consumption. Most of the experiments resulted that the communications over-heads inside cache-group had important role in performance of group-caching [21].

1.3. Cooperative Cache

1.3.1 Cooperative caching importance

As high-speed networks will allow the systems under the networks to access remote data as quickly as it looks like data is fetched from local server instead of main server. It reflects the idea of cooperative caching. Many machine distributed on a local areas network have cording cache files to gain more efficient overall cache file. Different simulation techniques were used to find the proper solution related the placement of cache of distributed servers to improve the speed of access that is improving read time response for which simple algorithm of cooperative caching are enough to find the appropriated performance gain in the system files access approach. So the high-speed networks had an opportunity for the remote clients to work closely in team to improve the file system performance. By the study we conclude that cooperative cache can reduce the read time responses by using near by workstations while simple algorithms can handle the access on the station of the client to server.

1.3.2 Cooperative caching research work

Further a proper mechanism should propose and implement by combining all the caching techniques such as cache consistency, cache invalidation, cache discovery, cache replacement algorithms to overcome the identified issues. This will become a challengeable task to overcome because the technology is changing rapidly in every single second, therefore whatever the mechanism that going to implement is should be very effective and stable for longer period of time and should adapt to the changes in technology.

1.3.2 Cooperative caching future

The amount of research work under process reflects that the cooperative cache is gaining an important role in all fields of networks like wireless Ad-hoc networks, wired networks, wireless sensor networks, social wireless networks, social multimedia wireless networks and also in microchip processing to increase the performance of overall network data sharing with low cost and high speed.

1.3.3 Group Cooperative Caching

The concept of group cooperative caching is to share the memory of local servers with the domain servers to increase the access speed of contents and minimizes the delay of fetching, while each group of cache is under checking process to make sure the updating of the contents to end user.

2. Literature Review

2.1 Cache Application

The cache application had get importance because for the factor of fast data accessing and processing from the memory used in system which impacts the system performance. Some of the areas mentioned below where cache applications are vast in use for better performance.

2.1.1 Mobile technology

In modern era mobile computing is also the main emerging technology. It allows data transmission which may be consists of text, audio or video through a system or any kind of wireless devices without having to a particular physical line. The major problems in mobile technology is computing a cache management which refers to data accessibility, high bandwidth consumption, delay of data access and package loss, letdowns in databank servers and data server capability are current problems in mobile computing cache. Some of researches have pointed above disadvantages that are happened paid to some disasters in cache reliability algorithms, cache replacement algorithms, cache finding algorithms and cache admittance control. These days there are several of researches are disclosed that narrates to the cache and its management in mobile computing technology. As an outcome of those approaches, different mechanisms, algorithms and tools are suggested to boost the cache managing in mobile computing but some of the revealed issues are still under discussion. [22]

2.1.2 Computer System Technology

Caching is basically a skill that has been involved in several areas of the computer and also to networking engineering for some time. Whereas various different ways of caching and its implementation. Caching is the process of storing repeatedly used data in an easily available locality so that period and resources are retained because data does not have to be recovered from the actual source. With times as well as resources are always a superior in the networking and computing industry. The existence of cache is almost in machines high performance. In detail, the processor of every computing device (Switches, routers, tablets, mobile phones and PCs) takes benefit of caching to increase the speed of memory access. Surely, a number of PCs consuming cache technology in the CPU shows the significance of caching at the hardware level too. Web browser is the same application of caching in the terms of computer system technology. So most of usually used browsers use caching like web caches used for loading demanded objects so the same objects should not be retrieved again from web server. This process is identified as object caching.[23]

2.1.3 Network Technology

Problems related to data recovery, optimization of application interchange in wide area network has become the strategic resolution of selection for enterprise globally. By using optimization approach for data, the traversal of wide area network, this is the core solution for optimization. The distance between the user and data is the core affecting issue in data retrieval procedure. Enhancement is provided by optimizing the WAN data traffic, but the most ideal solution is that it retrieval should not be done if data is not in need. Different form of caching approaches can be used for this type of data retrieval. All it is because the reply time is important, so in larger distance network optimization must include different optimization techniques like protocol optimization, management of bandwidth and compression but also different form of caching approaches such as object and byte caching. In all that byte caching is considered a common in optimization in WAN while object caching is an important module presently lacking in most of the solutions. So from results it shows that caching minimize the broadcast of data over the wide area network (WAN) and allows immediately access of data, both factors will straight improve response (reply) time and utilization of bandwidth. The purpose was to know the importance of caching in all field related to network and system.[23]

2.2. Cooperative Caching Application and Research

2.2.1 Mobile Environment

Data enabled mobile devices present usage and wireless-enabled data applications have promoted in present mobile ecosystem new content broadcasting models have promoted usage in present data enabled mobile devices while using wireless enabled data applications. So giving free access to the local connected devices to share the server load and access the data and ignore the application cost of downloading and sharing such mechanism is also known as cooperative caching in wireless networks Carrying mobile in work places like in public parks, university campus, markets, malls, airport terminals and other public spots get connected to Social Wireless Networks would be automatically formed by using the devices by ad hoc wireless connections. Those devices list includes Apple's iPhone, Google's, Androids, Amazons and other electronic vendors etc.

2.2.1.1 Group Base P2P in Mobile Environment

The recent widespread development of peer to peer (P2P) of wireless mobile communication technologies like IEEE 802.11 and other coupled the fact that computation power and storage of most mobile devices are improving in fast pace, A new information sharing paradigm known as P2P information access has rapidly taken change. The mobile clients can communicate among themselves to share information rather then having dependency on the connectivity to server [13]. As many researchers implemented the same technique of cooperative caching on the networks like web environment and all those implementations are the levels of system [2]. So for improving the access of data is done through cooperative caching technique gets importance [12].Similarly there is rapid growth in mobile communication technology. Mobile ad hoc Networks (MANETs) are the popular solution where you don't have network infrastructure. MANETs can be extended by connecting other devices that may be physically wired or in wireless network like Internet. The cooperative caching can improve the performance of system in wireless P2P networks such as hoc networks and mesh networks do. Somehow these all very high level studies leave many design and implementation issues which are still unanswered.

2.2.2 Wireless P2P Network
- ✓ Purpose: Find the place to cache the data.
- ✓ Proposed Idea: A novel Asymmetric cooperation cache approach

2.2.2.1 Asymmetric cooperation cache approach.
On every node data request is transmitted to the cache layer but replies are only to the nodes that are in need to cache data which are mostly intermediate nodes.

2.2.2.1.1 Purpose:

- *Reduce overhead of coping data between the user space and kernel space.*
- *Also allows data pipeline to reduce the end to end delay.*

2.2.2.1.2 Study Reflection.

- After applying on different MAC layers such as 802.11 based ad hoc network and multi interference and multi-channel based mesh network on the performance of cooperative cache. Results shows that these approaches outperform symmetric approach are traditional 802.11 based ad hoc networks by removing most of the processing overhead.
- Data Access delay is reduced in the asymmetric approach compared to the symmetric approach in mesh network because of data pipeline.

2.2.2.1.3 Method used:

- Adopting Cache node selection approach and considering caching over heads to maximize the benefits of cache on different lays of MAC.
- The Greedy cache placement algorithm is proposed.

2.3 Modules

1) Cooperative Cache Module:

   As many routing algorithm provide the hop count information among source and destination, coding the data path for each data item reduces bandwidth and power consumption because nodes can obtain data using fewer hops.

2) Cache and routing module:

   - ➢ Cache and routing modules should be tightly coupled for implementation of cooperating cache at the network.
   - ➢ Caching functionality can be added by modifying routing modules.

3) Asymmetric approach Module:

   Three layers are identified

   1) *Forwarding the request message*

      Messages generated by applicants passed to cache.

   2) *Determining the cache node*

      To send request to next hop cache layer will wrap original message with new destination address.

   3) *Forwarding the data reply.*

The packet is received and processed hop by hop all nods on the path from the requester to the data server.

2.3.1 Chip Multiprocessor

As with respect to hardware feature of microprocessor architects designed the Micro chips to improve the access and processing to get full control over data execution, so cache also have portion of key role in hardware point of view for chip micro processors that where logical accessing of data should be started.

2.3.2 Wireless Multi Media Sensor Network

To understand some real life security issues to cooperation in Wireless sensor networks (WSN) there are some issues always in mind to establishing cooperative network. As in any computer wireless network the goal is defined by security measures in enhancing operation and access. The different security goals in cooperative networks are related to data integrity, authentication, confidentiality and availability. Some of the major problems in such networks can me summarized in following categories that are

- Hackers and malicious users accessing week nodes
- Interruption technique can be used in which the hacker cuts the link and thus messaging that the node unavailable in sensor networks.
- Code injection in which maliciously adding the codes to the device that help the hackers.
- The interception technique in which hackers threatens the wireless networks.
- Unauthorized access to the WSN by transmitting data packets with the contents.

Similarly the different techniques can be used in wireless censor networks like fabrication attach approach, information gathering approach, Node insurrection, traffic mining, routing information, selective filtering, cooperative communication technique, in which user get the most available recourses and injecting sensor node.

Capacity and availability plays an important role in enhancement of network throughputs.

2.3.3 Ad-hoc Network

Cooperative cache concepts have key role in improvement of system performance in Ad-hoc network. As the concepts of mobile communication and social wireless communication networks are mostly based on Ad-hoc networking concept that automatically reflects the importance of cooperative cache in simple Ad-hoc network. So a study shows that sharing data between nodes can improve the overall performance in peer-to-peer network. From the studies it comes that the novel technique relies on two main ideas.

- At every node on cache layer receives the cache data request
- The node that needs cache data which is intermediate node on the cache layer will receives the replies

Different methodologies used for implementation such as CCA (Cooperative Cache Agent), cooperative cache daemon (CCD) and A cooperative cache supporting library (CCSL).

2.3.3.1 Wireless

So giving free access to the local connected devices to share the server load and access the data and ignore the application cost of downloading and sharing such mechanism is also known as cooperative caching in wireless networks.

3. Future of Cooperative Caching

In the field of networks and communication the importance is performance with fast access. The speed of data access is major point on which each network performance and enhancement depends. The availability of data in time where client needs in very short time in the network with a load is another important issue always thinking of adding clients. So as these all issues are there in our communication technology so to overcome cooperative caching technique can somehow overcome the issue of data access and speedup the network performance by sharing data in local domain instead of remote domain. Hence more innovative solutions should be proposed to overcome the issues by considering the facts that addresses the development of new approaches for the management of mobile cache. For identified issues a proper scheme should also be proposed by implementing the technique of combing all the methods used for caching such as consistency, discovery, invalidation and replacement. As the technology changes rapidly in a seconds so it will be a challenging task to overcome, so the proposed mechanism should be stable for a long time period and must be very effective which can be adoptive to the coming technologies.

4. Summary

- Cooperative Caching (CC) has main role in improving the performance in retrieving of data in mobile networks for mobile clients.
- Cooperative caching can reduces the server load by allowing its local client's for cache misses and can be handled by the other shared clients.
- Cooperative Caching can save communication cost, bandwidth and energy.
- Can be used as new technique for eliminating redundancy that will reduce the space requirements for inter network storage. This can be performed on the entire system at multiple levels.
- To decrease the memory size of caching data the compression technique can also be used.
- Applying compression only to the already cached objects that are accessed frequently can solve the problem of computational overhead in compression.
- Instead of using remote memory data can be fetched and accessed from local memory domain.
- Instead of going to remote memory for cache miss, local cache can be checked.

5. Case Study

The qualitative approach is used for finding the concept of cooperative cache in different fields of computer networks as well as in computer design architecture. Similarly the role of cooperative cache in enhancement of data access has been analyze and also finding out the different techniques used for concepts of cooperative caching in mobile as well as sensor networks.

6. Future research areas

From the recent studies we come to know that the cooperative caching can improve the performance of system in wireless networks such as hoc networks and mesh networks do. Somehow these all very high level studies leave many design and implementation issues which are still unanswered. While by study it shows that issues related the implementation of cooperative caching concept in networks and in system design still under consideration for the areas like cache memory size, cache locality, data consistency, cache cost, placement, identification of the area to be placed, replacement (which data block should be deleted) and writing policy that what and when it can store and for how long.

7. Conclusion

Over the past few decades, the use of applications to enable business processes has evolved significantly. What was just the once a nice-to-have is currently a ordinary fastener that exists at the core of commerce, education, and other operations across the world. As application usage has greater than before, the reply time has turn into more and more significant with good explanation. So waiting is considered a time wasting and money wasting with production lost. Affecting factors for reply time today include overcrowded WAN pipes, ineffective/informal protocols and latency due to extended distances between data and user. All these factors are exacerbate as applications and data resources are consolidate, centralized, or outsourced. So in a lot of cases delays translate into irritated users.

8. References

[1] Beal, Vangie. *WeboPedia.* Property of QuinStreet Enterprise. 2017. http://www.webopedia.com/TERM/C/cache.html (accessed March 10 March, 2017).

[2] Chang, Yi-Wei Ting and Yeim-Kuan. *A Novel Cooperative Caching Scheme for Wireless Ad Hoc Networks: GroupCaching* . Thesis, Department of Computer Science and Information Engineering , National Cheng Kung University , 701 Tainan, Taiwan R.O.C. : IEEE International Conference on Networking, Architecture, and Storage (NAS 2007), 2007.

[3] Chi-Yin Chow, Alvin T. S. Chan. "Group-based peer-to-peer cooperative caching in mobile environment." *IEEE Journal on Selected Areas in Communications.* IEEE Xplore, February 2007.

[4] "Cooperative Caching in Ad Hoc Networks." *4th International Conference on Mobile Data Management.* Melbourne, Australia.: MDM 2003,, 10 Sep 2009. pp.13-28.

[5] Drepper, Ulrich. *WiKIPEDIA.* February 24, 2017. https://en.wikipedia.org/wiki/CPU_cache (accessed March 10, 2017).

[6] Hartman, Prasenjit Sarkar and John. *Efiicient Cooperative Caching using Hints.* Research Paper, Department of computer Sciences, Universty of Arizona, Tucson: Universty of Arzona, 4.

[7] HoneyPot ITC Software Solutions and Services. *Cooperative Caching in Wireless P2P Networks :* *Design, Implementation and Evaluation.* Transactions on parallel and distributed systems, HoneyPot ITC Software Solutions and Services, IEEE, Feburary 2010.

[8] Jichuan Chang, G.S.Sohi. "Co-Operative Caching for Chip Multiprocessor." *Computer Architecture ,2006,ISCA 06,33rd International Symosium On* . IEEE xplore, Feburary 2006. 38.

[9] Jichuan Chang, Gurindar S.Sohi. *Cooperative Cache partitioning for chip Multiprocessors.*Research paper , ICS , Universty of Wisconsin-Madison, Universty of Wisconsin-Madison, 2014.

[10] Madhukar R.Konpuly, C.Greg Plaxdon,Rajamohan Rajaramn. *Placement algorithms for Heirachical cooperative caching* . Thesis, Department of Computer Science , Universty of Texas, Austin: Universty of Texas, June 1999, 586-595.

[11] Manolopoulos, Nikos Dimokas · Dimitrios Katsaros · Yannis. "Cooperative Caching in Wireless Multimedia Sensor Networks." *Mobile Netw Appl.* Springer Science + Business Media, LLC 2008, 11 June 2008.

[12] P.Kuppusamy, Dr.K.Thirunavukkarasu,Dr.B>Kalaavathi. "A Review of Cooperative Caching stratigies in Mobile Ad Hoc Networks." India: International journal of Computer Applicationsa, September 2011.

[13] Prashant Kumar, Naveen Chauhan, LK Awasthi , Narotham Chand. *Proactive Approach for Cooperative Caching In Mobile Adhoc Networks.* Hamirpur: International Journal of Computer Science issues, 2010.

[14] Surgi Srinivas Guod, (M.Tech), Shankar Thalla,M.Tech. "Distributed Cooperative Caching in   Social Wireless Networks." *International Journal of Computer Trends and Technology(IJCTT)* 14   (August 2014).

[15] Torres, Gabriel. *Hardwaresecrets uncomplicated the complicated.* sep 12, 2007. http://www.hardwaresecrets.com/how-the-cache-memory-works/3/ (accessed March 10,   2017).

[16] Yan, Chow Chi. *Peer to Peer Cooperative Cache in Mobile Environment.* Thesis, Department of Computing , Honkong Polytehnical Universty , HonKong: Honkong Polytehnical Universty ,   Decemeber 2004, 200.

[17] Stone, Dan. *Chron.* LLC Hearst Newspapers. 2017. http://smallbusiness.chron.com/important-   processor-cache-69692.html (accessed March 10, 2017).

[20] ichael Pietroforte Wed, J. 1. (2013, July Wednesday). 4sysops. Retrieved 03 Saturday, 2017, from https://4sysops.com: https://4sysops.com/archives/group-policy-caching-in-windows-8-1/

[19] Implemeting the cache. (n.d.). Retrieved March 11, 2017, from http://people.cs.pitt.edu: http://people.cs.pitt.edu/~melhem/courses/1502p/unit6-cache.html

[18] M.S. Smith, L. S. (2011, May 05). Bright hub. Retrieved 03 11, 2017, from http://www.brighthub.com: http://www.brighthub.com/computing/hardware/articles/32165.aspx

[21] Wang Zuo, S. F. (20-24 April 2009). Group-caching for NoC based multicore cache coherent systems. Design, Automation & Test in Europe Conference & Exhibition, 2009. DATE '09. (p. 262). IEEE.

[22] Tennakoon1, T. (2017). Effective Cache Management in Mobile Computing Environment. *e-ISSN: 2320-0847 p-ISSN : 2320-0936* (pp. pp-318-321). colombo,Sirlanka: American Journal of Engineering Research (AJER).

[23] Blue Coat Systems Inc. (2013). *BLUE COAT,A TECHNICAL REVIEW OF.* Retrieved March Tuesday, 2017, from https://www.bluecoat.com: https://www.bluecoat.com/documents/download/9457735e-8603-40a1-a566-11d3f62aae8a/c645fb5d-746c-4be3-a40c-ae1cbce54141

[24] Michael D. Dahlin, R. Y. (November 14 - 17, 1994). Cooperative caching: using remote client memory to improve file system performance. *OSDI '94 Proceedings of the 1st USENIX conference on Operating Systems Design and Implementation.* onterey, California —.